[redacted]

Discover PHILIPPIANS

by
Neva Evenhouse

revised by
Sylvia Boomsma

FAITH ALIVE®
Christian Resources

Grand Rapids, Michigan

Unless otherwise indicated, Scripture quotations in this publication are from the HOLY BIBLE, NEW INTERNATIONAL VERSION, © 1973, 1978, 1984, International Bible Society. Used by permission of Zondervan Bible Publishers.

Cover photo by SuperStock

Faith Alive Christian Resources published by CRC Publications.

We welcome your comments. Call us at 1-800-333-8300 or e-mail us at editors@faithaliveresources.org.

ISBN 1-56212-152-9

10 9 8 7 6 5 4 3

Contents

How to Study

The questions in this study booklet will help you discover for yourself what the Bible says. This is inductive Bible study—no one will tell you what the Bible says or what to believe. You will discover the message for yourself.

Questions are the key to inductive Bible study. Through questions you will search for the writers' thoughts and ideas. The prepared questions in this booklet are designed to help you in your quest for answers. You can and should ask your own questions too. The Bible comes alive with meaning for many people as they discover for themselves the exciting truths it contains. Our hope and prayer is that this booklet will help the Bible come alive for you.

The questions in this study are designed to be used with the New International Version of the Bible, but other translations can also be used.

Step 1. Read the Bible passage several times. Allow the thoughts and ideas to sink in. Think about its meaning. Ask questions of your own about the passage.

Step 2. Answer the questions, drawing your answers from the passage. Remember that the purpose of the study is to discover what the Bible says. Write your answers in your own words. If you use Bible study aids such as commentaries or Bible handbooks, do so only after completing your own personal study.

Step 3. Apply the Bible's message to your own life and world. Ask yourself these questions: What is this passage saying to me? How does it challenge me? Comfort me? Encourage me? Is there a promise I should claim? A warning I should heed? For what can I give thanks? If you sense God speaking to you in some way, respond to him in a personal prayer.

Step 4. Share your thoughts with someone else if possible. This will be easiest if you are part of a Bible study group that meets regularly to share discoveries and discuss questions. If you would like to learn of a study group in your area or if you would like more information on how to start a small group Bible study, write to Discover Your Bible, 2850 Kalamazoo Ave. SE, Grand Rapids, MI 49560 or to P.O. Box 5070, STN LCD 1, Burlington, ON L7R 3Y8.

Introduction

Do you want to be a star? Paul's letter to the Philippians can tell you how! Oh, not like those stars primping behind dressing-room doors or lounging in spacious Hollywood mansions. Quite the opposite, in fact. Paul's stars shine in homes, offices, factories, schools, hospitals, neighborhoods—even in prisons—spreading pure light among the crooked and depraved.

Perhaps more than any other apostle, Paul had learned the art of shining in the darkness. When he wrote this letter, he was imprisoned and awaiting trial for his life. Even under those circumstances, Paul let his light shine by sharing the gospel with those around him and continuing his correspondence with the churches he had begun.

In his letter to the Philippians, Paul shares much of what he learned about living the Christian life, standing firm, and behaving as one of heaven's citizens. The tone of his letter is loving and personal; the Philippians, whom Paul calls his dear friends, brothers, his joy and crown, held a special place of affection in his heart. As you will see, they were especially supportive of Paul through their financial help, prayer, commitment to the gospel, and friendship.

Though written to first-century Christians, Paul's letter is timeless. It speaks to all believers everywhere of the importance of standing firm in the faith, deepening a personal relationship with Christ, living in humility and unity with other believers, and grasping the peace and joy each child of God can experience in Jesus Christ, regardless of circumstances. It teaches children of God how to be blameless and pure, how to shine like stars, holding out the word of life and lighting their corner of a dark world.

Glossary of Terms

Benjamin (tribe of)—one of the twelve tribes, or sections, of the Old Testament Israelite nation (see also *Israel*). Paul was born into this elite tribe.

Caesar's household—those in Rome's imperial service, probably included palace officials, secretaries, clerks, servants, dependents, and slaves.

Day of Jesus Christ—the day when Christ will return.

circumcision—removal of the foreskin of the penis. God commanded the Old Testament Jews to do this as an outward sign that they belonged to him, and as a symbol of the cutting away of sin from their lives. In the New Testament, circumcision was replaced by baptism.

deacons—church members chosen to collect and distribute gifts of money and other items, and to serve those with special needs.

depraved—corrupt, wicked, perverted.

drink offering—wine or some other drink poured out as an offering to God or a pagan god. Old Testament Jews sometimes poured a drink offering over an animal or other item that was to be sacrificed.

Epaphroditus—a Philippian man who had worked beside Paul and was very dear to him. He probably carried Paul's letter from Rome to Philippi.

faith—taking God at his word; being "sure of what we hope for and certain of what we do not see" (Heb. 11:1). True saving faith is a combination of knowledge and confidence: a sure knowledge by which one accepts as true all that God has revealed in the Bible, and a confidence that all one's sins are forgiven by Christ.

gospel—comes from the Greek word meaning "good news." The gospel is the message that God's Son, Jesus Christ, took the punishment for our sins upon himself, dying on the cross and rising again for the salvation of his people; that he ascended into heaven; and that he will someday return.

grace—God's kindness, undeserved and unearned favor, and forgiving love.

Hebrews—the Jews (see also *Israel*).

humility—a modest sense of one's own importance or rank; lack of competition or desire for recognition.

Israel (people of)—the Jews, the Old Testament chosen people of God, descended from Abraham, with whom God formed a covenant to be God to all his descendants. The Old Testament tells the story of the Jews, the nation from which Jesus eventually came.

Jesus Christ—the second person of the Trinity, equal to and one with the Father and Holy Spirit. Jesus is the sinless Son of God, who gave his life as a payment for sin.

legalistic righteousness—outward sinlessness, concerned with technical obedience to the letter of the law, rather than Jesus' law of love.

overseers—also called elders; church members responsible to see that the word is preached and order is maintained in the church.

palace guard—members of the elite imperial regiment, the emperor's palace and body guards.

Pharisees—Jewish men who dedicated their lives to the Jewish Law of the Old Testament by learning its every letter, teaching it, and keeping it in perfect outward obedience. Though some of them may have had good and sincere motives, Jesus (whom they hated for abolishing the Law) condemned them for their hypocrisy.

righteousness—perfect obedience to God's will and moral standards. God regards as righteous through Christ those who accept Jesus' sacrifice on their behalf, which takes away the guilt of their disobedience.

sacrifice—offering a precious gift (or oneself) to someone else. The Bible says that the guilt of human sin cannot be removed without the sacrifice of a life. In Old Testament times sacrificial animals represented the giving of life. In the New Testament, Christ gave his life as the final sacrifice in payment for sin.

saints—from the Greek word meaning "separated unto God." In the New Testament it refers to all who live by faith in Jesus Christ.

salvation—eternal freedom from death and punishment for sin. God gives salvation to those who in repentance and faith receive Jesus Christ as Savior and Lord.

Spirit (or Spirit of Jesus Christ, or Spirit of God)—the third person of the Trinity, equal to and one with the Father and Son. The Holy Spirit convicts of sin, works true faith in believers' hearts, and empowers them to live holy lives. His presence in believers' hearts guarantees that they will receive all of God's promises.

Timothy—a convert of Paul's who became his assistant and his "beloved son" in Christ. He traveled extensively with Paul and was with him when he wrote to the Philippians.

Word of life—the gospel (see *gospel*).

Lesson 1

Philippians 1:1–11

From the First Day Until Now

1. Philippians 1:1–2

a. How does Paul describe himself and Timothy? What does this tell us about them?

b. To whom is Paul writing?

c. What does Paul want for his readers? What does this mean?

2. Philippians 1:3–8

a. How does Paul regard the Philippians? Why does he feel this way?

b. What is Paul confident of? What do you think this means?

3. Philippians 1:9–11

a. What is Paul praying for in these verses?

b. Why does he want this for the Philippians?

c. According to verse 11, what would be the final result of Paul's prayer for the Philippian believers? For God?

4. Philippians 1:1–11

a. What does this passage tell us about Paul and his relationship with God? What seems to be the motivating force in Paul's life?

b. What do these verses tell us about the Philippians? About their relationship with Paul?

c. Why is Paul certain that the Philippians' faith is genuine and will continue?

Lesson 2

Philippians 1:12–30

To Live Is Christ

1. Philippians 1:12–14

Paul probably wrote this letter during his imprisonment in Rome. He was allowed to live in his own rented house, correspond, and receive visitors, but was chained to a Roman guard at all times.

a. According to Paul, how did his circumstances help spread the gospel? By what means did this happen?

b. Why do you think Paul wanted the Philippians to know this? What could they learn from it?

2. Philippians 1:15–18

a. What do these verses tell us about those who preached Christ while Paul was in prison? What did each group hope to gain?

b. What can we learn about Paul from these verses?

3. Philippians 1:18–20

a. Why did Paul rejoice? What did he expect to happen?

b. Why was he so confident about this?

c. What was his primary desire as he thought about his own future?

4. Philippians 1:21–26

a. How did Paul view life and death? What were his reasons for viewing them as he did?

b. What did he expect would happen to him? Why was he so confident of this?

5. Philippians 1:27–28

a. What did Paul want the Philippians to do?

b. Why was unity important for the Philippians?

c. What will result from their Christian behavior?

6. Philippians 1:29–30

a. What was the struggle Paul and the Philippians were going through?

b. How do you think Paul wanted them to view this struggle?

7. Philippians 1:12–30

a. What can we learn from these verses about Paul and his relationship to Christ?

b. Read through this passage once more, observing Paul's attitude toward:
—his own future —life and death
—his work —the gospel of Christ.
What can we learn from his example?

Lesson 3
Philippians 2:1–11

Christ's Attitude . . . And Ours

1. Philippians 2:1–2

a. In your own words, what did Paul want the Philippians to do?

b. According to Paul, why should they do this?

2. Philippians 2:3–4

a. What kind of behavior destroys unity? What sort of behavior promotes unity?

b. What attitude toward others did Paul encourage? What effect does one's attitude have on the unity of the entire group?

c. How might the Philippians have carried out Paul's instructions? How can believers obey them today?

3. Philippians 2:5–8

a. What did Paul say about Jesus in these verses?

b. What did these facts reveal about Jesus' attitude?

c. Why did Paul point out these things? How might such a mindset affect the Philippians' daily lives and relationships?

d. What affect should Jesus' attitude have on Christians today?

4. Philippians 2:9–11

a. What was the result of Jesus' obedience?

b. What is Jesus' present position, according to Paul?

c. For what purpose did this occur?

5. Philippians 2:1–11

a. Make a list of qualities Paul's readers should strive for and pitfalls they should avoid.

b. On the basis of these verses, how would you define humility?

Lesson 4

Philippians 2:12–30

Shining Like Stars

1. Philippians 2:12–13

a. The words "so then" or "therefore" point to the reason Paul's readers are to obey. To what do they refer?

b. What is Paul asking his readers to do? What is their responsibility with regard to their salvation?

c. What is God's part in their salvation?

2. Philippians 2:14–16

a. How does Paul want his readers to behave?

b. What will result from this behavior?

c. Describe the contrast between the world and the children of God living in that world. What can believers offer the world?

3. Philippians 2:17–18

a. In what way might Paul be "poured out" for the Philippians?

b. How does he feel about that?

4. Philippians 2:19–24

a. What does Paul say about Timothy in these verses?

b. What do these verses reveal about Paul?

5. Philippians 2:25–30

a. Describe the character and work of Epaphroditus.

b. What was his relationship with Paul? With the Philippians?

c. What did Paul want the Philippians to do? Why did he want them to do this?

6. Philippians 2:12–30

a. What do these verses reveal about the attitudes of Paul, Timothy, and Epaphroditus? How do they compare with the attitude described in verses 1–11 and 14?

b. How can the modern church "shine like a star" among today's crooked and depraved generation? How can individual believers shine?

Lesson 5

Philippians 3:1–21

Pressing on Toward the Goal

1. Philippians 3:1–3

a. What did Paul want to protect the Philippians from?

b. Why was he so strong in condemning these people?

c. On what grounds did he call them to rejoice?

2. Philippians 3:4–9

a. Describe the kind of confidence Paul speaks of in verses 4–6.

b. What was Paul's attitude toward those things on which he once depended?

c. Why did he no longer depend on them? What was his new source of confidence?

3. Philippians 3:10–11

a. What did Paul want a deeper knowledge of?

b. What would result from this?

4. Philippians 3:12–16

a. Describe Paul's focus in his desire to know Christ.

b. What do you think is the "goal" of which Paul spoke in these verses? What is the "prize"?

c. Describe the attitude or "view of things" which Paul wanted his readers to have. Was Paul an optimist or a pessimist? Explain.

d. What was Paul urging his readers to do?

5. Philippians 3:17–21

a. According to these verses, what can believers gain by observing each other? What is the value of having models to imitate?

b. How did Paul describe the "enemies of the cross"?

c. What is the basic difference between these enemies and people who live according to Paul's pattern? What is the destiny of each group?

6. Philippians 3:1–21

a. What did Paul learn from his own experiences about faith, confidence, and security?

b. After a person comes to know Jesus, what attitudes, interests, and expectations should he or she have?

Lesson 6

Philippians 4:1–23

Standing Firm

1. Philippians 4:1

a. In your own words, what did Paul want the Philippians to do?

b. Why should they do this?

2. Philippians 4:2–3

a. What problem did Paul address?

b. What did he ask of those involved?

3. Philippians 4:4–7

a. Describe the believer's mindset, based on what Paul says here.

b. How should the Philippians have handled whatever situation they might have faced?

c. What does Paul say about the peace of God?

4. Philippians 4:8–9

a. On what did Paul direct his readers' thoughts? Their actions?

b. What did he say they were to do?

c. What will result from doing these things?

5. Philippians 4:10–13

a. In what did Paul rejoice and why?

b. How do you think Paul would define "contentment"?

c. How did he come to this understanding of contentment?

6. Philippians 4:14–20

a. What do these verses reveal about the relationship between Paul and the Philippians?

b. Why is it important for believers to give to others? What results from their generosity?

7. Philippians 4:21–23

a. How does Paul close his letter to the Philippians?

b. What do these verses reveal about Paul and the situation in Rome?

8. Philippians 4:1–23

a. Summarize how a believer's relationship to Christ makes a difference in his or her attitudes, human relationships, thoughts, and reactions to circumstance.

b. What rewards of the Christian life are mentioned in this chapter?

9. Philippians 1–4

Summarize what you have learned about the Christian life from your study of Philippians.

Evaluation Questionnaire

DISCOVER PHILIPPIANS

As you complete this study, please fill out this questionnaire to help us evaluate the effectiveness of our materials. Please be candid. Thank you.

1. Was this a home group ___ or a church-based ___ program? What church?

2. Was the study used for
   ___ a community evangelism group?
   ___ a community grow group?
   ___ a church Bible study group?

3. How would you rate the materials?

   Study Guide
   ___ excellent ___ very good ___ good ___ fair ___ poor

   Leader's Guide
   ___ excellent ___ very good ___ good ___ fair ___ poor

4. What were the strengths?

5. What were the weaknesses?

6. What would you suggest to improve the material?

7. In general, what was the experience of your group?

Your name (optional) ______________________________

Address ______________________________

8. Other comments:

(Please fold, tape, stamp, and mail. Thank you.)

Faith Alive
2850 Kalamazoo Ave. SE
Grand Rapids, MI 49560-0300